Inside Machines

Tractors
and Other Farm Machines

David West

WINDMILL
BOOKS ™

Published in 2018 by **Windmill Books**,
an imprint of Rosen Publishing
29 East 21st Street, New York, NY 10010

Designed and illustrated David West

Cataloging-in-Publication Data
Names: West, David.
Title: Tractors and other farm machines / David West.
Description: New York : Windmill Books, 2018. | Series: Inside machines | Includes index.
Identifiers: ISBN 9781499483321 (pbk.) | ISBN 9781499483260 (library bound) | ISBN 9781499483147 (6 pack)
Subjects: LCSH: Tractors–Juvenile literature. | Agricultural machinery–Juvenile literature.
Classification: LCC TL233.15 W47 2018 | DDC 631.3'72–dc23

Manufactured in the United States of America

CPSIA Compliance Information: Batch BS17WM: For Further Information contact Rosen Publishing, New York, New York at 1-800-237-9932

Contents

All-terrain vehicle

ATV stands for all-terrain vehicle. ATVs are also known as quad bikes. They are used by farmers around the world. They are ideal for crossing the rugged landscapes of sheep and cattle farms. They also tow trailers that can be used to carry animal feed or injured sheep.

A sheep farmer uses an ATV to pull a trailer over the rough terrain of a mountainous sheep farm.

Inside an All-terrain vehicle

Fuel tank

Bale of hay

Handlebars

ATVs have handlebars like bikes to steer them. The **throttle**, **clutch**, and brake lever are all on the handlebars.

Engine

ATVs use motorcycle engines to power them.

Suspension

The suspension has big springs and oil-filled **dampers** for each wheel.

Tires

The knobbly tires grip the rocks and muddy surfaces of the rough terrain.

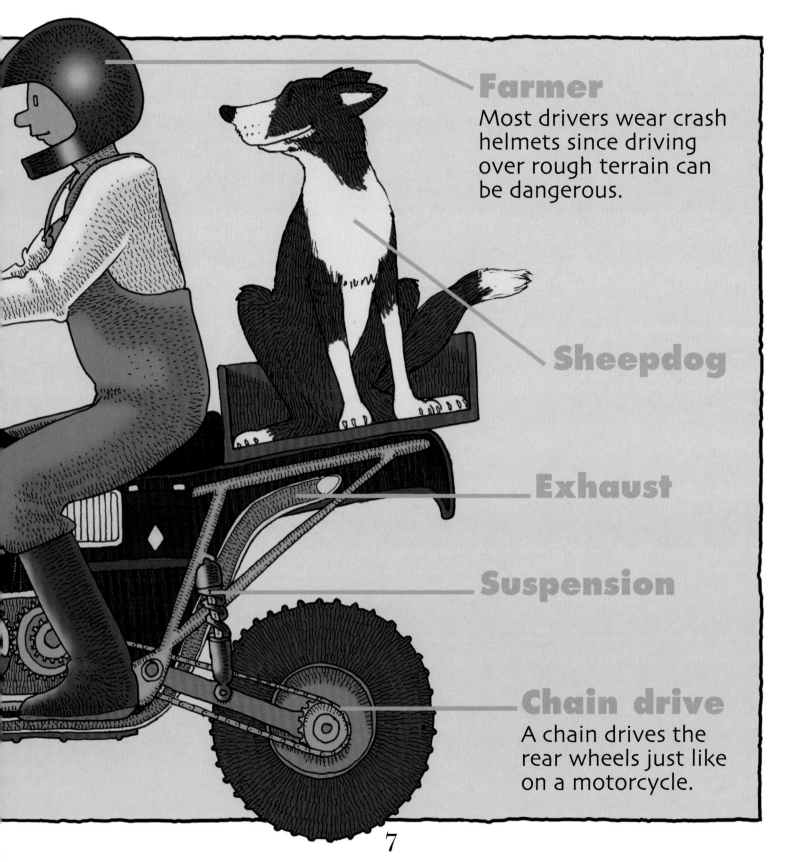

Farmer
Most drivers wear crash helmets since driving over rough terrain can be dangerous.

Sheepdog

Exhaust

Suspension

Chain drive
A chain drives the rear wheels just like on a motorcycle.

7

Tractor and baler

Tractors are the workhorses of the farm. They are used to haul a variety of machinery such as plows and balers. Tractors have very big engines that power all four wheels. Their tires have large treads which dig into soft earth to make them grip.

This tractor is pulling a round baler. The machine gathers up hay and rolls it into bales. This is done after the crop, such as wheat, has been collected by a combine harvester (see page 12).

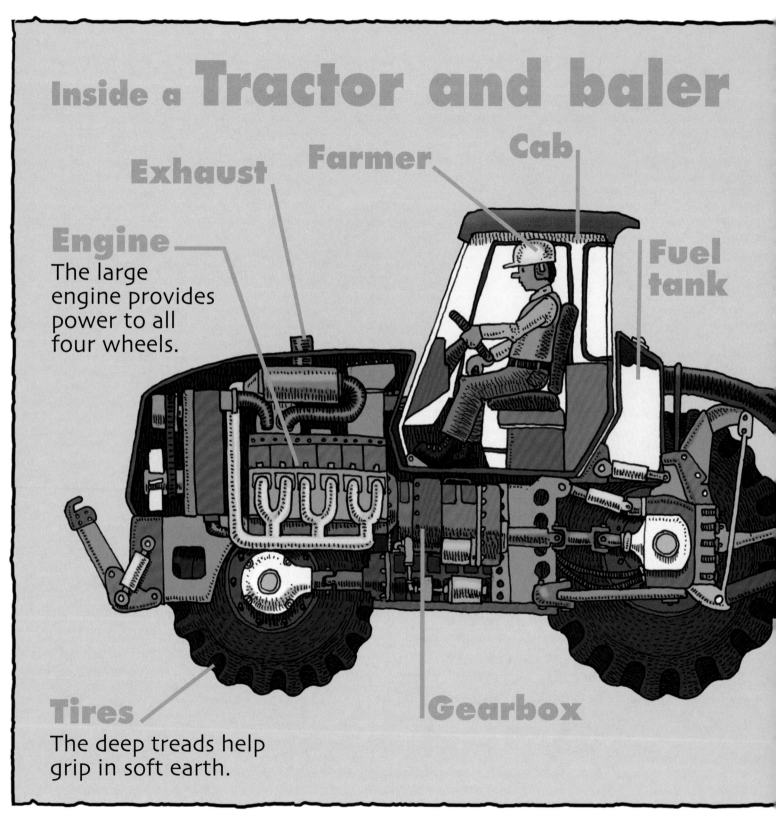

Inside a **Tractor and baler**

Farmer

Cab

Exhaust

Engine
The large engine provides power to all four wheels.

Fuel tank

Tires
The deep treads help grip in soft earth.

Gearbox

Engine

The baler has its own engine.

Round baler

The round baler makes round, or rolled, bales.

Rubber belt

Hay is rolled up inside the baler using rubber belts.

Tailgate

When the bale is ready the tailgate opens up and ejects the bale.

Pick up

This roller picks up the hay from the ground.

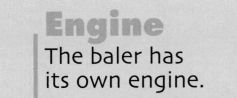

On large fields a combine harvester can only carry some of the grain. When the grain tank is full the grain is emptied into special trucks. This can happen while the combine is still harvesting.

Combine harvester

These specialist machines are designed to cut a crop, such as wheat, oats, rye, or barley, and then shake the grain free. The grain is collected in the grain tank. The rest, the stems and leaves, are dropped out of the back. They are later collected into bales of hay (see page 9).

Inside a **Combine harvester**

Driver

Cab

Threshing drum

Here the crop is transferred to the straw walker.

Reel

The crop is gathered by the reel and cut at its base by the cutter bar.

Stone trap

Any stones collected fall in here.

Head auger

The crop is directed to the grain conveyor.

Crop

Cutter bar

Grain conveyor

Grain tank
Grain is delivered here by the grain **auger**.

Grain auger

Auger
This auger transfers the grain to a truck.

Engine

Straw walker
The lighter stems and leaves are shaken along to the end as the heavier grain falls through it.

Stems and leaves

Chaff

Fan
This blows air to clear the light **chaff** from the grain.

Sieves
The grain gradually falls through the shaking sieves.

15

Plants on this farm have been grown in rows at a certain distance apart so that the crop sprayer's wheels fit between them.

Crop sprayer

On some farms special crop-spraying machines are used. They apply **pesticides** and **fertilizers** accurately so that the plants are not damaged. Special sensors on the boom keep the spray heads at the right height.

Inside a **Crop sprayer**

Farmer

Cab

Spray nozzles

Engine

Wheels

Large wheels keep
the vehicle high
off the ground.

Steps

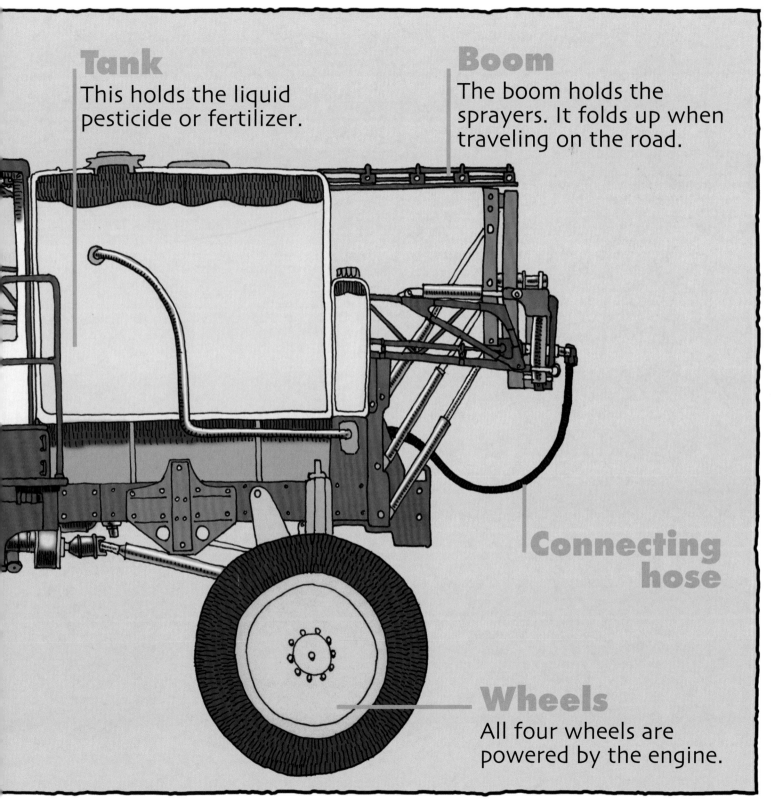

Tank
This holds the liquid pesticide or fertilizer.

Boom
The boom holds the sprayers. It folds up when traveling on the road.

Connecting hose

Wheels
All four wheels are powered by the engine.

Horse trailer

Some farms breed horses for racing and other events. Specialized trucks are used to transport the horses and riders to the racecourses and arenas by road. In addition to stables, horse trailers also have a kitchen, shower, lounge, and a bedroom.

Some of the biggest horse trailers can carry up to eleven horses.

Inside a **Horse trailer**

Storage for horse supplies

Air vents

These let fresh air into the stables.

Rear door

The rear door folds down to make a ramp for the horses to enter the trailer.

Storage for animal feed

Stables

Batteries

22

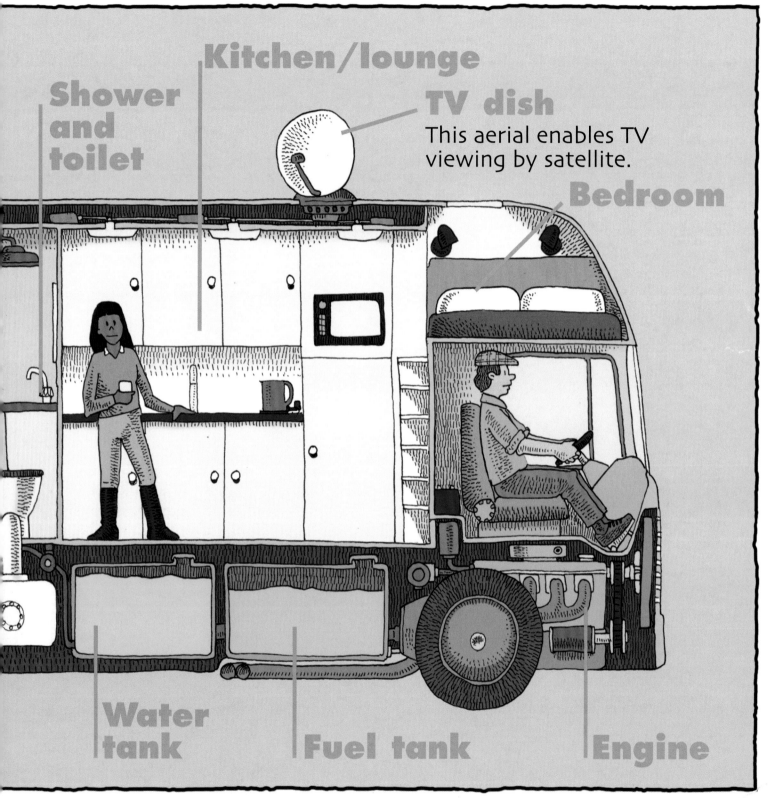

Shower and toilet

Kitchen/lounge

TV dish

This aerial enables TV viewing by satellite.

Bedroom

Water tank

Fuel tank

Engine

Glossary

auger
A conveyor that uses a rotating screw blade inside a tube to move liquids or grain.

chaff
The husks of corn or seeds separated by a harvester.

clutch
A device that disengages the power when changing gear.

damper
A device in a vehicle's suspension designed to absorb bumps.

fertilizer
Nutrients to help plants grow.

pesticide
A substance that protects plants from pests.

throttle
A device that controls the flow of fuel to an engine.

Index